CROWN OF LIGHT

CLAIRE ELIZABETH GROSE

Copyright © 2019 by Claire Elizabeth Grose

Compiled and edited by Michael Grose and June Kennedy

All rights reserved. No portion of this publication may be reproduced, stored in a retrieval system or transmitted in any form by any means – electronic, mechanical, photocopying, recording, or any other –except for brief quotation in printed reviews, without the prior written permission of the publisher.

Unless indicated otherwise, all scripture quotations in this book are from the following source:

The Good News Bible: The Bible in Today's English Version (TEV) © 1976 by the American Bible Society. Used with permission.

ISBN 978-0-6486884-0-2

Author contact information - clairegrose.heartmatters@gmail.com

Version 1.0

DEDICATION

This book is dedicated to Michael and Andrea,
Precious gifts from my Lord

CONTENTS

DEDICATION IV

CONTENTS V

PREFACE VIII

ACKNOWLEDGEMENTS X

> PART ONE 1
> > MY DAILY PRAYER 4
> > SOLACE 5
> > SPRING 6
> > SPIRIT SHOWERS 7
> > MOON 8
> > MORNING FOG 9
> > BRING YOUR HEART 10
> > MAJESTIC WONDERS 11
> > NIGHT FALL 14
> > PURE ELEGANCE 15
> > HEAVEN'S GIFTS 16
> > SERENADE 17
> > SUN 18
> > MAJESTIC RAYS 19
> > AROMAS COOL 20
> > GOD'S LOVE COMING DOWN 21
> > DAWN 22
> > SHADOWS BLUE 23
> > BUDS IN TIME 26
> > SCARLET VIEWS 27
> > SPIRIT CALL 28
> > COME TO ME 29
>
> PART TWO 30
> > BE STILL 33
> > MY HEART'S DOOR 34
> > BEAUTIFUL ONE 35
> > YOUR LOVE MAKES ME LOVE 36

MY SMALL VOICE	37
IT'S ENOUGH	38
AUTUMN LEAVES	41
FOUNTAIN OF HOPE	42
LIFE'S JOURNEY	43
CLOSE AS CLOSE	44
DEAR ONE	45
BLESSINGS	46
FAITH AND GRACE	49
GOLDEN MOMENTS	50
CLAIM HIS LOVE	51
DAY AFTER DAY	52
SAVOUR THE MOMENT	53
TWO ON THE LINE	54
UNTIL MORNING CALLS	57
WHISPERED PRAYER	58
YOUR WINGS ARRIVE FOR SHELTER	59
QUIET TIMES	60
THROUGH THE VALLEYS AND HILLS	61
BE MY CONFIDANTE	62
CALL ME BACK	63
ROCKY ROAD	64
STEPPING STONES	65
IN SUNSHINE AND IN STORM	66
EMPTY DAYS	67
WHEN YOU CALL MY NAME	68
PART THREE	69
GO ALONG QUIETLY	72
FRAGILE LIVES	73
FOLLOW HIS LOVE	74
ONE SO TRUE	75
THE VALLEY FLOOR	76
TRANSPARENT LIVES	77
CROWN OF LIGHT	80
GUIDED BY THEE	81

LOOK UP	*82*
HEAVEN'S HOLY ONE	*83*
SUPREME CALM	*84*
VEIL ME IN YOUR BEAUTY	*85*
PART FOUR	*86*
HIS HOLY GROUND	*89*
FRUIT OF THE VINE	*90*
HEART OF LOVE	*91*
SURRENDER	*92*
BLESSED ONE	*93*
I'M YOURS FOREVER	*94*
THE ONE TRUE VINE	*95*
HEAVEN'S LOVE	*98*
HIS BRIDE TO BE	*99*
MORNING AND EVENING STAR	*100*
THE LIGHT OF THE WORLD	*101*

PREFACE

Two things I just wanted to say about this book are, why I started writing and how I came by the title.

I grew up in the 1950's-1960's in Adelaide, South Australia, my life was pretty simple but wonderful. I was very lucky to have a secure family life, and my Mum and Dad brought the family up to treat others with respect, do the right thing, be courteous, and respect your elders. We had a strict upbringing and even as adults our parents never criticized us but encouraged us to do our best in life. They were "Aussie battlers" but we always managed to make it through the tough times!

They were people of integrity and cared about others and instilled that into our family.

Church was a big part of our lives growing up. We went to Sunday School at an early age and progressed up through the appropriate groups as we got older.

Youth groups, camps and church anniversaries were all important to the whole family. We competed in church sports teams, basketball and tennis with other parishes across Adelaide. Life-long friendships were in the making and cherished golden memories to look back on that would never fade.

Bible stories, hymns and choruses were all part of getting to know Jesus. This nurturing finally led me to the day Jesus came knocking on my heart's door. Being filled with the Holy Spirit is something I will never forget and the overwhelming power of His love that filled my whole being and propelled me to the front of the hall to give my heart to Him. No words can fully describe the joy I felt. That was in February 1968, I was 14 years of age. He has been my Shining Light ever since, and lives within me always.

So I thank my beautiful Mum and Dad for the way they raised me and for the foundation of knowing Jesus' love.

It was in His love that I started to write, in the autumn of 1993. My journey has brought me to this book "Crown Of Light". The title came to me when I was thinking of God in His glory and majesty and how He is the "Light of the World".

"I am the light of the world," he said. "Whoever follows me will have the light of life and will never walk in darkness". John 8:12.

This is an offering from my heart to yours, reflecting on His divinity and greatness and His gift of grace and mercy to all who will believe in Him.

The journey through this book covers His beautiful gift of mother earth, the joy and wonder of it; His perfect love for strength and peace; the wonderful calm He will bring into your life if you ask Him; the celebration of what God's love can do for you if you open your heart to Him; His promise of eternal life for all who will believe that He died on the Cross for us and on the third day after His death was raised to life by His Father in Heaven.

The poems reflect the everyday feelings and emotions that we feel as we meet the challenges of life and how the great magnitude of God's love can help us rise above them.

I pray you will seek His eternal counsel in your everyday life and receive His grace and mercy through the pages of Crown of Light.

Many of these writings have been my first words of whispered prayer, so much that I have been moved to write them down at once and continue on in His wonderful and absolute love.

Together we write as He provides my inspiration.

All glory to Him, my precious Lord Jesus. Thank you for touching my soul, you are the only one who can!

ACKNOWLEDGEMENTS

My heartfelt thanks to my beloved family, my Mum and Dad, Lilly and Kenny, and my siblings Jeanette, June, Carol, Gloria and Lynne, for their never ending encouragement and support to me in finishing this book. It has been a journey we have travelled together, and we are so blessed that we share His love.

To the rest of my family, so precious to me; you all mean so much.

To Michael and Andrew for your continual support to me in fulfilling my passion of writing poems for the Lord to help others through His word.

To Michael for overseeing this book, thank you!

To Peter Mulraney (accomplished author) for his guidance and advice for starting me off on this journey and also for his help in configuring the cover.

A huge thank you to Junie for editing my poems and the coffees we enjoyed along the way.

To Joy for her Crown of Thorns drawing, you have an amazing gift, thank you. To my friends and church families, thank you for your love and support.

Many thanks to Michael, Andrea and Robbie for photographs.

To my beautiful sons, Michael and Andrew, thank you for loving me, and I am so glad He gave you to me. I will love you forever. To your partners Andrea and Bianca and also my grandchildren, I love you all so much.

To you the reader, thank you for picking this book up and I pray you will find His peace and love on the pages ahead.

May He shower you all with His love and blessings.

PART ONE

"…You are clothed with majesty and glory;
you cover yourself with light…"

Psalm 104 : 1, 2

CROWN OF LIGHT

YOU EMBROIDER THE EARTH WITH YOUR SEASONS…

MY DAILY PRAYER

Be with me, stay with me,
Close by my side,
Fill me with your peace and love,
So my spirit shall surely fly
To the heights in your love,
As only you can give,
Prepare me for this day ahead,
So in me you'll always live.

SOLACE

Lord, my soul feeds on beautiful dusk
As waning light calls moon,
Sky and sea merge as one
As the veil of night looms.

Perfect peace is all around
I feel a calm within,
Gentle breeze upon my face
As daylight suddenly dims.

The sea is calm and quiet
As evening falls around,
Time for rest and slumber
In your peace and love I found.

Your arms of shelter hold me close
As I drift off to sleep,
Cares I've thrown to the wind,
Stay close to me for keeps.

SPRING

Grateful thanks to you adorned
From morning prayers as day is born,
Early mist to Heaven ascends,
Leaving warmth 'til daylight ends.

Joyful life erupts with Spring
As earth gives birth to seeds within,
Kaleidoscope of colour explodes,
Exquisite blooms burst forth on show.

Rainbow colours are everywhere
Permeate joy to every stare,
Wealth in peace and calm they give
Restores the soul so man can live.

In gratitude for gardens lush,
And sweet perfumes on thermals rush
To fill our senses how divine,
We thank you Lord for Spring in time.

SPIRIT SHOWERS

Spirit showers that sparkle and shine
Fall on this heart of mine,
Washing me clean with joy divine,
Refreshes my soul time after time.

Thank you Lord for your Spirit showers
And your divine Heavenly power
That keeps you by my side,
Anywhere at any hour.

Thank you that your Spirit showers
Clear my thoughts and soul,
My faith renewed once again
For you have made me whole.

I feel your wondrous love and joy
Sending Spirit showers,
My soul responds to your love
Like an opening flower.

MOON

Lord, beautiful moon, made by you
Serenely she sits afar,
Poised so perfectly above
You placed her with the stars.

Like diamonds she dances on the sea
In awe we gaze in wonder,
What a gift to behold
The how and why we ponder.

Her soothing light spreads far and wide
Nurturing plants below,
Cocooned and cradled in the earth
Seeds begin to grow.

Her radiant glow speaks to my soul
Soothing deep within,
Cares and woes forgotten now
Her light will never dim.

MORNING FOG

Quiet bliss as fog rolls in
Covering sea and land,
Profound peace fills my soul
As I stand on dampened sand.

Thoughts are lost in the haze
As landscape becomes a blur
Lapping ripples pat the shore
The only sound to be heard.

Landmarks are out of view
From the fog that's hanging still,
Sun does its best to shine
But through the fog it never will.

Shells embedded in the sand
That the tide left far behind,
Waiting for the tide's return
And the journey beyond the "blue line".

I just can't believe how surreal that moment was,
Standing on the beach in the morning fog,
Thank you Lord for the peace that came to me
Just like it came to you, on the shores of Galilee.

BRING YOUR HEART

A flower dancing in the wind
Softly speaks without a word,
Such a beautiful thing,
The Lord I want to serve.

Find peace in His gardens
Such rapturous love He gives,
He speaks through Mother Nature,
The world belongs to Him.

So bow in admiration
To the one who made all things
Upon this precious Earth,
Just bring your heart to Him.

MAJESTIC WONDERS

Lord, Dawn and Sunset are the jewels in your Crown,
They arrive without a sound,
You command them every day to show,
Your hand displays them that I know.

Marking birth of day and night time rest,
Majestic wonders; our hearts are blessed,
They bring you oh so near,
Majestic wonders that appear.

Divine Creator of all things,
We give you praise oh Lord you bring
The rolling seas and snow capped peaks,
"Help us save your Earth" we sing.

Dawn in orange; a stunning sight,
Heavenly colours that mass the sky,
She's the best dressed in all the world,
Now golden Sunset bids farewell.

CROWN OF LIGHT

YOUR BEAUTY...
OUR JOY...

"...the earth is filled with your blessings."

Psalm 104 : 13

NIGHT FALL

Rolling hills sit quietly
Dusted in gold and mauve,
Misty fog rolls silently
Blocking them from show.

Setting sun slips out of view
To the other side,
Fading light escapes the sky
Kissing day goodbye.

Chill of evening settles in
I pull my collar high,
Sparkling stars begin to shine,
I give a thankful sigh.

The King of Kings is in control,
His earth spins another turn,
I feel Him close at night fall,
For Him my glad heart yearns.

PURE ELEGANCE

The perfume of God so sweet and divine
From all His flowers on the vine,
Exquisite they bloom for us to smell,
Born as tender buds that swell.

Though their beauty richly formed,
Yet when they wilt they are reborn,
To give us joy in sight and touch,
Pure elegance from God above.

HEAVEN'S GIFTS

Smile into a flower,
Breathe deep its scent within,
Carry that memory through the day
So sweetly made by Him.

Look longingly at a sunset,
Be filled with joy divine,
His colours made in Heaven
To thrill this heart of mine.

Soak in the calm of the ocean
When His moon sparkles and shines,
Its light dancing on the surface
Goes deep to this soul of mine.

Feel His sun upon your skin
And His breeze through your hair,
That's Mother Nature smiling,
Heaven's gifts from Him so fair.

SERENADE

Serenade me with your rain
As she gently cascades below,
So sweet it sounds to my ears
To hear the rain drops flow.

Mother Earth is washed all clean
Softly bathed in water streams,
Drops of moisture wash the trees,
Pearly beads dance on their leaves.

Racing down the window pane
Drums a steady sweet refrain,
Heaven's music loud and clear
Warms my soul from One so dear.

Soaking rain sends me to sleep,
The Saviour's arms I'll always seek,
Calm and peace wash over me,
Heaven's rain drops running free.

SUN

Horizon gives birth to sun
As dawn spills through my window,
Shadows fade away with light
As sunbeams come to life.

Threads of light fill my room
As I wake from evening slumber,
Time to start my daily plan,
What it will bring I wonder.

Lord, I love how I can talk to you
As day goes passing by,
Always be by my side
As sun spans open sky.

Soon enough it's time for dusk
As sun bows down in shades of musk,
Silence calls the end of day
As by my bed I kneel to pray.

MAJESTIC RAYS

Fresh sea breeze upon my face
As I walk along the beach,
In bare feet I kick the sand
While the sea silently speaks.

My soul feels His hand,
My spirit stirs inside,
A comfort unspeakable,
I feel Him by my side.

Golden threads stretch through the clouds
Connecting to the sea,
Spreading out so perfectly
In divine harmony.

The hazy beams in perfect form
Touching horizon blue,
Sun's majestic rays display
Dawn's breathtaking view.

AROMAS COOL

Close your eyes be still and calm,
He will soothe you with His perfumed balm,
So sweet the oil to anoint you so,
To restore your soul so it will grow.

His perfect love in abundance full,
Drifting through aromas cool,
Sparkling waters ripple and shine,
Thrill my soul time after time.

Fragrance sweet flows over me,
His glorious face I surely see,
Takes me to the heights unknown,
My Lord's perfume I surely know.

GOD'S LOVE COMING DOWN

Stormy skies in the west
Now on their way,
Sunset bows on the horizon,
Filtering her rays.

Like fingers they reach for earth
To touch the coming dusk,
So perfect in formation,
Love it so; I must.

Like a crown in the sky
Sun shines behind the clouds,
Threads of light a wonder,
That's God's love coming down.

Golden light adorns the clouds
Looking dark with rain,
Stormy sky now drifts away,
Leaving golden end of day.

DAWN

Birth of day so fresh and new
As time unfolds from scarlet views,
Shrills and whistles ride the breeze
Now dawn is here they're safe and free.

Beautiful dawn she stretches high
In ruddy shades she sweeps the sky,
Dodging puffy clouds around
By breezes on their courses bound.

Shadows flee as dawn arrives,
Morning mist floats to the sky,
Heaven's scents drift through the air,
Delights from our Master's hand so fair.

SHADOWS BLUE

Lord, all things lovely are you,
From green slopey glades to skies of blue,
Forest pines to mountain hues
Your world comes into view.

Your eye is made of beauty,
How glorious your forms,
You made Mother Nature
For me to adore.

Your touch so soft as velvet,
Still powerful in time,
Reaching out to heal and mend
The wounds of life that bind.

When my heart's in valley deep
Or lost in shadows blue,
Take me to your mountain top,
My home is there with you.

CROWN OF LIGHT

YOUR LIGHT...
MY GUIDE...

"Your word is a lamp to guide me
and a light for my path."

Psalm 119 : 105

BUDS IN TIME

We are but buds in time
As we grow in His love divine,
Speaking to the soul within,
We only have to look to Him.

To feel the comfort of His open arms
And to receive His blessings of peace and calm,
We only have to ask for these gifts
That will lead us to eternal bliss.

So like the sweet bud on the vine
Responds to the warmth of daily sunshine,
Grows into a beautiful bloom,
Our faith will blossom if we give Him room.

SCARLET VIEWS

Scarlet views thrill my heart
As dawn arrives on time,
Her beauty warms my soul each day
While I wait for sun to shine.

Coolness in the air is fresh
And dampness hangs around,
Clouds hug the horizon,
Today's here safe and sound.

My favourite time of the day
When all is fresh and new,
Looking from my window
I see His scarlet views.

Dawn brings her calm and beauty
No matter what betides,
I feel you close beside me,
Give me strength to ride the tide.

SPIRIT CALL

How blessed I feel to be your own,
You've touched my heart with love,
My soul it soars with joy divine
To your heights above.

To feel your Spirit close and warm
To prompt my hand to write,
You shroud my thoughts with heaven's glow,
You shower me with your light.

Your Spirit fills my heart with joy
Bathed in waters sweet,
Inspiration floods my mind,
I'm at your mercy seat.

I thank you Precious One above
For your Spirit call,
And writing every word with me,
You surely are my Lord.

COME TO ME

I love it Lord when you come to me
To still my mind, my thoughts,
Calmness arrives like a veil
To soothe and quieten my all.

Your presence follows so serene
I wait before you still,
Healing and soothing floods within,
My need you surely fill.

Time fades away I'm in your peace
I'm drawn towards your light,
Love divine fills my soul,
I'm humbled in your sight.

So come to me, stay with me,
Guide me on my way,
I need to meet you every day,
Your light will pave the way.

PART TWO

"But my trust is in you, O Lord; you are my God.
I am always in your care; …."

Psalm 31 : 14, 15

STEP OUT ...
WITH GOD...

BE STILL

Thank you Dear One for this moment,
I am still and quiet to hear your voice,
For this moment peace and calm reside in me.

Listening for You,
Waiting for your touch,
Going to that quiet place known only by you,
We meet.

Serenity claims me,
Allowing your voice to be heard
And your presence to be felt.

All thoughts are hushed as I surrender
To your beckoning
For peace, to be still,
For lips to be silent.

Shrouded in your Spirit call,
My soul is plunged into divine love
In its purest form,
Flowing from you in Heaven.

I bow down before you Blessed One,
Holy Eternal Father,
My Lord and my Master,
All glory to you forever.

MY HEART'S DOOR

When I look into your eyes
Great love I see within,
You fill me with the deepest joy
That makes my soul sing.

When I feel your presence near
Such warmth surrounds me so,
Your Spirit stirs my soul so deep
Only you divinely know.

May you see before your sight
The youth you called before,
When years ago you came to me
And knocked on my heart's door.

So thank you Lord for touching me
And calling me your own,
Make me worthy of your love,
In me you've made your home.

BEAUTIFUL ONE

Beautiful One, Holy One,
Come to me and shine
Your glorious beam of Light
Into this heart of mine.

Shower your love into my life,
A love that never ends,
To fill my heart with peace and calm,
The kind your Spirit sends.

Beautiful One, Holy One,
I bow down and worship you,
Thank you for loving me,
You make me feel brand new.

YOUR LOVE MAKES ME LOVE

Your love makes me love
When my heart warms to a soul,
It's you reaching out
To one of your fold.

Your love makes me love
When I'm focused and still,
You shroud me in your peace and calm,
My need you always fill.

Your love makes me love
When troubles rage,
I'm in your care,
So to you I pray.

Even though I can't see you
My faith is strong and true,
Thank you for loving me
I'll bow down loving you.

MY SMALL VOICE

Thank you Lord for hearing my voice
And for giving me the choice
Of loving you and being your child,
And your touch that makes me smile.

With all the prayers that are continually sent
At day's beginning until day's end
You still hear my small voice of prayer,
So thank you Lord for what we share.

Thank you for being so faithful to me
And for giving me strength
When I have the need,
And for all the things that I ask of Thee.

The miracle that you hear each prayer
From hearts down here to your Throne up there,
Where you reside in your heavenly calm,
Answered prayer feels like soothing balm.

IT'S ENOUGH

Sometimes Lord it's enough
Just to think of you,
When words fall silent for prayer,
My heart still longs for you.

It's enough to close my eyes
And see you on your Throne,
Where you light up heaven
Your eternal home.

It's enough to believe
That you're my King of Kings
Who went all the way to Calvary
To save me from my sins.

Yes it's enough to say
"my Lord, how I worship Thee",
And kneel lowly before your Throne
And confess "Thou lives for me".

CROWN OF LIGHT

YOUR PRESENCE DEMANDS MY ALL ...

"You are the source of all life, and because of your light we see the light."

Psalm 36 : 9

AUTUMN LEAVES

For the nine months she carried me
She would never know,
If I would be in perfect form
'Til her time to birth me showed.

Cocooned I grew so silently
Through months of tears and sighs,
But when she held me tight that day
Tears of joy spilled from her eyes.

I relied on her for everything
When I first came to this world,
She cared for me so lovingly
In her hands my life she held.

But autumn leaves touch my soul
When they turn the colour gold,
A life of love was given up,
The years are gone to have and hold.

So when autumn leaves fell, God came for her,
A beloved life for Him,
She loved Him more than anything
And now in Heaven she lives.

FOUNTAIN OF HOPE

Springs of life shower on me
Spilling over my soul,
Tears will wash away in streams,
Bound for His Throne of Gold.

Vanishing over hills of light
Destined for rainbow skies,
Heartaches will disappear from view
When you trust Him with all your might.

There's only one fountain of hope for me
That's Jesus Christ, my Lord,
His eternal spring flows evermore
So we can live in one accord.

So refresh your heart in showers of love
That flow from the Lord of Life,
Take your share from the fountain of hope,
From Him the Eternal Christ.

LIFE'S JOURNEY

Some people cross our path
Just for a little while,
Like clouds drifting pass
On their course, mile after mile.

Some stay for a short time
And leave a flower on the heart,
Some stay for a life time
Joined together and never part.

Some stay long enough
To leave a scar that's open wide,
But there is only one
Who can soothe the pain inside.

Life can leave its footprints
On the heart, soul and mind,
But there is one so mighty
Who can mend the wounds we find.

The storm clouds overhead
That shake the peace within,
Have a word with the Prince of Peace,
Just give your heart to Him.

CLOSE AS CLOSE

Close as close our love must be
Forever more with you and me,
Down through the years of time
To always fill this heart of mine.

Keep me charged with life divine,
Come to me, be mine be mine,
Never leave me all alone,
Make my heart your heavenly home.

Seek me, find me, fill my soul,
Come close as close to make me whole,
Fill me with your love divine,
Holy One be mine be mine.

DEAR ONE

Dear One, that's what you are to me,
Dear One, in my prayers I say to Thee
"How sweet and beautiful you are,
You shine brighter than the stars".

Dear One, you're there when I need to talk,
You were mine before I could walk,
You gave me breath so I could breathe,
Dear One, thank you for loving me.

BLESSINGS

Blessings showered from the stars above
Can only be your heavenly love,
Peace surrounds my spirit inside,
Owned by you where you abide.

Dreams soar to the heights above,
Consumed in your love,
Transformed by your sight,
They emerge in your Light.

So thank you Lord for your blessings
That flow abundantly
And for touching my very soul,
You know my every need.

I NEED YOU ALWAYS LORD…

"The Lord is my light and my salvation;…"

Psalm 27 : 1

FAITH AND GRACE

You wait for me so constantly
A member of your family,
To have a chat at any time
And recharge this heart of mine.

Ever sweet your love descends
Upon my soul, your Spirit sends
Divine calm, hope and peace
That brings me to your Holy seat.

Keep me charged with life divine,
Your believers are the fruit of the vine,
To spread your word to all the world
To share your cup must be upheld.

So Lord Jesus keep me near,
Send your Spirit to calm my fears,
Clothe me in your Majesty,
When faith and grace bring you to me.

GOLDEN MOMENTS

Lose yourself in His love
When thoughts play tricks on you,
Find His inspiration,
Seek a different view.

Think of His mountain tops
Or a bud on the vine,
Find Him in a sunset,
His love you'll surely find.

Don't let earthly cares
Bring a chill to your heart,
Find His love around you
So you can make a new start.

To each and every day
Like the dawn is fresh and new,
Lose yourself in His great love,
Golden moments wait for you.

CLAIM HIS LOVE

Claim His love in every way
Call close the Son of Man,
Walk with Him, your path in life,
He'll lead you by the hand.

Challenges may come along,
His armour you will wear,
His loving arms will hold you firm,
Just seek His face so fair.

Claim His love in all you do
To make your world so bright,
Claim His strength to rise above
The challenges of life.

DAY AFTER DAY

My thoughts are hushed as I look above
Towards your realm of wonder and love,
I try to forget the struggle within
As I search for peace and strength to cling.

Your powerful touch will soothe my soul
And guide me when I'm frail and old,
Still wielding your arm of miracle power
That surges ahead hour after hour.

So thank you Lord for your love you bring
To any heart that welcomes you in,
And the peace you send from Heaven's domain
Be with me Lord, day after day.

SAVOUR THE MOMENT

Savour the moment
When His Spirit comes near,
It will fill you with joy
And dispel your fears.

Savour the moment
When He calls your name,
Kneel lowly before Him
You will never be the same.

Savour the moment when you stand in His house,
Be filled with His blessings as you sing and shout,
All glory and grace in His holy name,
Accept His love, you'll be so glad you came.

TWO ON THE LINE

Two on the line when it's time to pray
Two on the line when you can have your say,
The Holy One waits patiently
For the tiniest whisper "Lord come to me".

Just two for a quiet talk
Any troubles He will always sort,
Thank Him like you would a friend,
His love and peace He'll always send.

Ask for His daily help,
He is always there,
He'll never let you down,
His strength and wisdom He'll always share.

To every caller He never hangs up!
From our joys to our sorrows, He's carried that cup,
He wants us to be free, He'll take them all,
Just take the time and make that call.

OWN HIS GRACE AND MERCY...

"...In the shadow of your wings I find protection..."

Psalm 57 : 1

UNTIL MORNING CALLS

It's so good to escape the world
And immerse myself in your love,
To forget the cares of the day
And think of you above.

Patiently waiting for my call
We meet and no-one at all
Knows of our meeting and your tender care,
You are my Lord; my heart I share.

To put my life in your hands,
To surrender each day to your heavenly plan
As together we walk until soft shadows fall
When sleep arrives until morning calls.

WHISPERED PRAYER

When earnest prayer fans the night
  And whispers utter a plea,
Give me strength to fight the fight
  Oh dear Lord stay with me.

Tears choke in my throat
  As I struggle to hold them back,
The one thing that I'm praying for
  Is the strength that I lack.

I'm praying for your light to shine
  To help me find my way
On this treacherous road of life
When my heart lies heavy some days.

My whispers fall on your face
  That's so close to mine,
Your words of love sound in my ears,
  Your loving arms I find.

YOUR WINGS ARRIVE FOR SHELTER

Some days life isn't easy,
The peace I thought I knew,
My world is turned upside down
I've got to see this through.

I know I'm overshadowed
By emotion running free,
Racing thoughts make way ahead,
I'm only thinking of me.

My heart is wounded inside
But my head says "think of Thee",
My fragile state overwhelmed
But Calvary set me free.

Your wings arrive for shelter
There I know I must reside,
Time will heal the scars
Once more you're by my side.

QUIET TIMES

Always in quiet times
I see you before me still,
I'm focused on your voice again,
In need I want to kneel.

Your arm cradles me close
When I come to you we meet,
That's in the quiet times,
The loudest you always speak.

Keep me close in your love and trust
You can speak without a word,
Whisper close in my ear,
My cries are always heard.

Your eyes pierce my very soul
With the purest love to be found,
As I bow lowly before you Lord,
Please say for me there's a crown.

THROUGH THE VALLEYS AND HILLS

The trail of life leads a windy path
Through the valleys and hills each day we pass,
The weary days that we remember still
Will one day fade behind the hills.

Keep looking forward to sunshine ahead,
Our hopes and our dreams with Him we should share,
They may not always come to plan,
Just ask Him to help you understand.

Walking through the valleys and hills,
He'll be your guide and your shield,
Trust Him He's your heavenly friend,
His loving grace He'll always send.

BE MY CONFIDANTE

Come to me in fields of grey
When I feel the need to pray,
I whisper my cares to you,
You are my confidante it's true.

You never tire of my demands,
You're always ready with open arms
To carry the weight I cannot bear,
I love you because you're always there.

When my plans don't seem to show,
It's for a reason I should know,
Give me wealth in mind and soul,
Always keep me in your fold.

So thank you Lord for all your care,
With the contents of my heart I share,
Keep my faith strong and true,
Forever I'll belong to you.

CALL ME BACK

I'm glad I'm back where I should be,
Close to you,
Distracted by life
I lose sight of you.

Sometimes I step away from your arms,
I need your sea of calm
To wash over me and keep me safe,
To call me back when I fall from grace.

You never give up
You've got your eye on me,
And I'm so thankful
I'm where I should be:

Close to you.

ROCKY ROAD

Lord, sorry I desert you
When the going gets tough,
I wallow in my own anger
But it's time to say "enough".

Time to let it all subside
And flow away in streams,
I need your healing balm
That will soothe the pain in me.

All my thoughts and emotions
That control my life it seems,
I must steer away from this rocky road
To pastures lush and green.

Take my thoughts to mountain tops
Where the view is far and wide,
And coastal waters glitter and shine
So my heart can take to flight.

Your Throne of Eternal Love
Where you live in love divine,
Peace and calm reside within,
Your light will always shine.

STEPPING STONES

Life is full of stepping stones,
Some are rough and some are smooth,
Guide our feet to safety Lord
To dodge the ones that bruise.

The souls of our feet
That crack and split from toil,
With your precious healing balm
Anoint us with your oil.

So thank you Lord for smoother stones
Where the waters just slip away,
To leave us with a firm foot hold
So we can clearly find our way.

IN SUNSHINE AND IN STORM

Lord, shine your light to all the world
In sunshine and in storm,
Though shadows fall around us
You will heal a heart that's torn.

Don't focus on the pain within,
Lift your eyes look up to Him,
Look deep within His heavenly face,
You will receive His gift of grace.

Feel His tender love so dear,
His open arms will draw you near,
To hold you close next to His heart,
His love and yours will never part.

Those storm clouds will disappear
Leaving sunshine's rays of hope and cheer,
So you can face another day,
Take precious time to pray.

EMPTY DAYS

Empty days, my soul lies flat,
I feel no charge within,
What have I done to feel like this?
My heart still yearns for Him.

I've put my trust in the Lord so long,
My road has been mapped out,
I'm at the crossroads once again,
"Which way?" I want to shout.

"Keep the faith" rings in my ears,
Some days it's hard to do,
When empty days keep rising up
To hide the distant view.

So Lord Jesus hold me close,
Show me where to go,
Fill me with your peace and calm,
I know you love me so.

WHEN YOU CALL MY NAME

When you call my name from Eternity
It's then that I see you facing me,
With eyes that pierce my very soul,
No words can ever unfold.

When you call my name it makes me stop,
I lift my gaze to your mountain tops,
Where your glory speaks from the valleys and peaks,
I'm in awe at the way they speak.

At the thought of you, thinking of me,
The Holy Messiah I'm not worthy of Thee,
Sin and shame I see in me,
But the King of Kings wants to talk with me.

I can never repay what you've done for me,
On the day you gave me Calvary,
So thank you Lord for calling my name,
Because of your grace I will never be the same.

PART THREE

"But those who trust in the Lord for help
Will find their strength renewed.
They will rise on wings like eagles;
They will run and not get weary;
They will walk and not grow weak."

Isaiah 40: 31

HIS SOOTHING BALM...
WILL HEAL YOU...

GO ALONG QUIETLY

I need His great mercy every day of my life,
I know I haven't always done what was right,
Now I try to make amends
Through His Holy Spirit He continually sends.

To fill me with His wondrous love,
His never ending grace that He sends from above,
His forgiving heart that feels the hurt
From speaking words that should never be heard.

Pain and fear that leave a scar,
He walks with me however far,
He never gives up on my fragile life
When sometimes we don't talk from morn 'til night.

Life is a battle
We don't know what's ahead,
"Just go along quietly"
My Mum always said.

She also said make worries a "matter of prayer",
The Prince of Peace is ready to share,
He has time to listen to every word,
Our prayers are always heard.

FRAGILE LIVES

You see through our fragile lives
Each day as we pass the time,
Sometimes we wake to golden days
And some we seem to lose our way.

Forgive us for the times we miss
The moments of your heavenly bliss,
When your Spirit wants to smile inside
But we're too busy to recognize.

When your light beams shine on the heart
Your glorious love will never depart,
Calling to the human soul
Your precious love is joy untold.

So restore those fragile lives within
From shadows that crowd us in,
To sunshine in your golden rays
Reaching out to bless us each day.

FOLLOW HIS LOVE

Follow His love in all you do,
Take your lead from the King of Kings,
He is love for all mankind,
To you His grace He brings.

Follow His love in all you do,
Always trust Him in all you pursue,
Though His plans may be different to yours,
Keep your faith He will open doors.

When your heart is crushed by a spoken word
Remember "no cry ever goes unheard",
The King of Kings hears all we say,
He will give you strength along the way.

So follow His love in all you do,
His golden light will shine on you,
He'll live in your heart every day,
Our salvation He surely paid.

ONE SO TRUE

Some days when my heart feels blue
And I think "I won't see this through",
It's okay to turn inside
To look at myself and what do I find?

A peaceful glade with gently flowing streams,
Or confusion "is this a bad dream?"
A steep hill like a mountain to climb
Or a tangled branch on a curling vine.

There's only one place to leave the blues,
Place them in the hands of the One so true,
Because He knows my thoughts and plans,
He will see me through, He understands.

So take the hand of the Heavenly Father,
Walk in His footsteps, forever after,
He knows the wrangling of the human heart,
Always turn to His everlasting arms.

THE VALLEY FLOOR

I'll never give up though my heart lies flat
When I walk the valley floor,
The Lord seems a long way off
But seek Him I'll implore.

I feel His shadow over me
But His arms I long to own,
Never forsake me Lord
I can't live my life alone.

I crave for the mountain top
Where my heart soars in your love,
Golden moments strike my soul
And you shine like the stars above.

So walk with me through the valley floor,
Where the trail is narrow and dim,
Charge me with your light divine,
Dismiss these days within.

TRANSPARENT LIVES

Thank you Lord for your love divine
When we find we walk the line,
Things happen beyond our control
That rocks our very soul.

Faith in you can help us through
This fragile fight to the light in you,
Give us strength to carry on,
Your shoulder we can lean upon.

Use your hand that calmed the sea
To touch and heal what's wrong with me,
Make me whole and cleanse me through,
Thank you Lord for all you do.

SOUL SEARCHING...

"...I am the light of the world,"
he said. "Whoever follows me will have the light of life and will never walk in darkness."

John 8 : 12

CROWN OF LIGHT

Breathe on me your Spirit divine
Empower me in your love,
Let your sweetness flow within,
Streaming from you above.

Give to me eternal love
Your promise to all mankind,
Your gift to every believing heart
Who kneels before your shrine.

Shroud me in your calm and peace
To soothe my hurts and fears,
Bathe me in your oil so sweet
And wipe away my tears.

May I be a worthy soul
To wear your Crown of Light,
To shine so brightly in your realm
While your arms they'll hold me tight.

GUIDED BY THEE

Shroud me in your calm and peace
To quieten the fears that rise in me,
Remind me Lord I need not doubt,
You have my life all mapped out.

I just have to let my days unfold
And yield to your perfect mould
Why should I worry, you made all I see,
I should just let go and be guided by Thee.

When I think that no-one cares,
I should lift my eyes to your heavenly stare,
Your Holy face my focus should be
So my heart would always be guided by Thee.

Fill me with your light so deep
And keep me on track 'til at last I see
Your home above and Eternity,
Where I will always be guided by Thee.

LOOK UP

Look up to His realm above
And feel His majesty,
Lose yourself in His great love
For He has set you free.

Look up to His realm above
When things aren't going right,
Have a chat with the King of Kings,
Ask Him to hold you tight.

Look up to His realm above
When you're thankful to see the dawn,
He'll carry you through the day ahead
When you're feeling weary and worn.

Look up to His realm above,
He's waiting to catch your eye,
Just take that step, receive His love
From His glorious Throne on high.

HEAVEN'S HOLY ONE

Heaven's Holy One,
Shower me in your light,
Cast your shadow over me
That takes me to your heights.

Fill my soul with joy divine
And my heart with pure love,
Your eye is always upon me,
To your Throne I want to come.

So I can bring my cares and fears
To your Mercy Seat,
You take them all away from me
In a heartbeat!

Your beauty Lord is so divine,
You shine like the morning sun,
I'm so glad you came to me,
Heaven's Holy One.

SUPREME CALM

Your breath is the breeze upon my face,
The sun is your warmth from our embrace,
In the rain you gently wash away
My sin that left a tearful stain.

The clouds in the sky I cannot touch,
They pass me by in such a rush,
Like all lives that come and go,
Your will be done, that I know.

I need your supreme calm as I pass through each day
And try to do good along the way,
Forgive me when I trip or fall,
You always answer every call.

So shroud me in your supreme calm
In the shelter of your loving arms,
Hold me close to your majesty,
Breathe on me Eternity.

VEIL ME IN YOUR BEAUTY

Veil me in your beauty
Dress me in your love,
Help me to shine for you
Like the stars up above.

Veil me in your beauty
You made things great and small
From the tiniest seed to the tallest tree,
They existed at your call.

Veil me in your beauty
So my heart can beat with yours,
Some days it's weak and fragile,
Dispel its wounds and flaws.

So veil me in your beauty Lord,
Make me worthy to be your child,
Take my hand lead me on
So I can see your heavenly smile.

PART FOUR

"Father," he said, "if you will, take this cup of suffering away from me. Not my will, however, but your will be done."

Luke 22 : 42

CALVARY'S COST...
DIVINE LOVE...

HIS HOLY GROUND

Come to His Altar for sanctuary
From the weary days that you see,
Where there just seems to be rain all around,
Take your heart to His holy ground.

At His Altar you'll fall to your knees,
Your heart will feed on His calm and peace,
You'll surrender the many broken dreams
And ask forgiveness for hurtful deeds.

His Spirit will touch your very soul
As He carries you back into His fold,
Safe in His sanctuary of holy ground
Where His pure love is found.

To humbly receive His sacrifice cup,
To hear His voice of eternal love,
To wear His sacred robe of grace
That moment when you see His face.

So come to His Altar for peace within,
Any time of day you call for Him
He'll be in your heart forever more,
His holy ground is eternally yours.

FRUIT OF THE VINE

The holiest of times
The Fruit of the Vine,
When we come to share
In His Bread and Wine.

These Sacraments that we can partake,
Touches so deep that I must dedicate
My love for Him from that moment on,
Forgive me Lord for all my wrongs.

I am humbled and lowly as I eat the Bread,
I bow down before Him, and must confess
"Forgive me for the sinner you see,
Thank you Lord for Calvary."

When we share His Cup we are one with Him,
The Holiest of moments: my heart bows to Him,
My spirit flies before His Throne,
My heart you surely own.

To symbolize His great sacrifice,
So all the world will have eternal life,
The Fruit of the Vine, His bride to be
How lucky are we, His family.

HEART OF LOVE

Heart of love that's you
Beating from above,
Heart of love it's true
The Father sent His Son.

To give a life without sin
That loves and cares for us,
He suffered on Calvary's Cross
To surely show His love.

He is the Son of Man
Who taught us how to pray,
He carried His Cross to Calvary
He took our sins away.

His heart of love beats for the world
Every night and every day,
How can we ever show our love
That we never can repay?

So thank you precious Lord above
For your gift of Calvary,
I pray that every heart will call
The Son who set us free.

SURRENDER

Surrender to the King of Kings
For inner peace within,
He'll lift my cares and fears away
To make my heart sing.

He's standing right beside me
Though earthly eyes can't see,
But my heart it fills with wonder
At His love He gives to me.

To bow down at His mercy seat
Where He will set me free,
My soul will shine within His light,
It's where I want to be.

Shrouded in His peace and calm
My life I give to Him,
He'll come in His great majesty
To take me home with Him.

BLESSED ONE

You are dear Lord, the Blessed One,
Your love is ever true,
From the road to Calvary
To Eternity with you.

Blessed One your love so great,
You obeyed your Father's call,
Your sacrifice upon the hill
Will forever save us all.

Blessed One your healing power
From your hand that made the world,
You reached out to heal the sick,
Our broken hearts you healed.

Blessed One your light so bright
You shine brighter than the sun,
Thank you for loving us
So our heart's can beat as one.

I'M YOURS FOREVER

I'm yours forever Lord
Because you carried that Cross,
My sin you took away
So I would never be lost.

I'm yours forever Lord
You washed me white as snow,
The day you Baptised me Lord
My tears of joy sure flowed.

Your beam of Light went through my heart
It made me feel brand new,
Your Holy Spirit showered me,
My soul I gave to you.

THE ONE TRUE VINE

Sharing His Communion Cup
Solemn I become,
In remembrance for Christ Jesus,
Because He gave His love.

Our precious Lord Jesus,
Forever He will be,
The one true vine,
He took the Cross at Calvary.

The one true vine our Saviour
The foundation of mankind
Gave His life for us,
The branches of His vine.

Yes the one true vine of life,
Paid the supreme sacrifice,
Obedient to His Father,
Only Son of the Most High.

He loves us so much,
On the Cross was raised up high,
Now He lives for ever
Eternal; the one true vine.

CROWN OF LIGHT

HE ROSE...
HE LIVES...

"He is not here; he has been raised, just as he said..."

Matthew 28 : 6

HEAVEN'S LOVE

Heaven's love, the sparkling stars
That shine upon us from afar,
In wonder we look to the heaven above,
Shrouded in peace, calm and love.

His warmth it flows to all mankind,
The Lord's desire that we should find
His wondrous love for each of us,
Poured out for man from Calvary's Cross.

Lord, your heart aches for man to plead
"Father, Father, come to me,
Forgive me, help me, guide my way,
Bless my life from day to day".

Heaven's love flows through the sky
Filtering down to you and I,
So open your heart to the humble Christ
And receive from Him eternal life.

HIS BRIDE TO BE

His bride to be; the Church of the world
Will praise and worship with arms upheld,
To welcome Him with hearts full of love,
The Holy One calls His beloved to come.

His bride to be; His believers He'll see
Will worship and praise His Majesty
With songs of love that He will adore,
As we worship Him forever more.

His bride will reflect His shining light
As she stands before Him in His sight,
To present herself to His glorious Throne
When He takes her hand and claims her "His own".

She will wear the ring of Eternal Life,
Loves purest band, the Circle of Light,
To never let go of His Holy hand
When at His Altar forever she stands.

His eternal home He's prepared for His bride,
Safely arrived to be by His side,
Always together for Eternity,
His bride to be; His family.

MORNING AND EVENING STAR

Morning and Evening Star,
Reflection of your love,
Shining bright into my heart
From your realm above.

Your light will never dim Lord,
You shine for the world to see,
Upon my heart forever Lord,
You will always be.

Your Morning Star calls the dawn,
Your Evening Star calls the dusk
As you command,
Bow to you I must.

The wonder of the heavenlys
Touches hearts and souls,
Your glory shines above Lord,
Your message must be told.

THE LIGHT OF THE WORLD

The light of the world
He always will be,
In His power and glory
One day we will see.

His glorious light
Will shine forever more,
In heaven He lives
In wonder and awe.

His beloved reside
In His peace and love,
Where He sits on His Throne
At the right hand of God.

Yes the Light of the World
He always will be
King of Kings and Saviour
For all Eternity.

ALSO BY CLAIRE GROSE

This is Claire's first book of inspirational poems to help others through the challenges of life.
They are inspired by God's love which is for everyone.

ABOUT THE AUTHOR

Claire worked as a Government Public Servant in the Lands Department, Adelaide, South Australia until she married and became a mother of two boys.

She later returned to the work force during which time she gained a "Living Hope" certificate which influenced her need to help others.

Through this and personal experience she found herself inspired by God's love to put pen to paper.

www.ingramcontent.com/pod-product-compliance
Lightning Source LLC
Chambersburg PA
CBHW050319010526
44107CB00055B/2310